Letters from a Young Father

Letters from a Young Father

poems by

Edoardo Ponti

Book layout by Olyvia Ashley
Cover illustration by Nick Bantock

Library of Congress Cataloging-in-Publication Data
Names: Ponti, Edoardo, 1973–author.
Title: Letters from a young father : poems / by Edoardo Ponti.
Description: First edition. | Pasadena, CA: Xeno Books, [2018] | Includes
   bibliographical references and index.
Identifiers: LCCN 2018002833 | ISBN 9781939096036 (alk. paper)
   ISBN 9781939096067 (ebook)
Subjects: LCSH: Father and chld—Poetry. | Parenthood—Poetry. | Life—Poetry.
Classification: LCC PS3616.O618 A6 2018 | DDC 811/.6—dc23
LC record available at https://lccn.loc.gov/2018002833

The National Endowment for the Arts, the Los Angeles County Arts Commission, the Ahmanson Foundation, the Dwight Stuart Youth Fund, the Max Factor Family Foundation, the Pasadena Tournament of Roses Foundation, the Pasadena Arts & Culture Commission and the City of Pasadena Cultural Affairs Division, the City of Los Angeles Department of Cultural Affairs, the Audrey & Sydney Irmas Charitable Foundation, the Kinder Morgan Foundation, the Allergan Foundation, the Riordan Foundation, and the Amazon Literary Partnership partially support Red Hen Press.

First Edition
Published by XENO Books
An imprint of Red Hen Press
www.redhen.org/xeno

To Papà,
I tried so hard to turn you into the parent I yearned for
I never took the time to appreciate the father you were.

CONTENTS

Letters from a Young Father

Introduction

What a remarkable book this is. In *Letters from a Young Father*, poet and filmmaker Edoardo Ponti has given us a haunting, deeply moving and celebratory collection of poems that is truly unlike anything I know—a book of poems addressed to his unborn child that echoes both Yeats's famous poem "A Prayer for My Daughter" as well as Rainer Maria Rilke's exquisite and timeless volume, *Letters to a Young Poet*.

Edoardo Ponti's *Letters from a Young Father* is a journal in poetry, each of these elegant and meditative poems having been cast in the form of a letter addressed to the poet's child—a poem for each week of his child's coming to term, the forty weeks leading to birth. A powerful diary of both self-reflection and autobiography, this book becomes most urgently a hymnal of hopes as well as a handbook of intimate instructions for charting a path for the life ahead. Quietly, inevitably, *Letters from a Young Father* reveals itself to be also a book of prayers, psalms and songs for every new child due for arrival in our world, as each page is intricately stitched with this poet's delicate revelations of his many learned—and hard-earned—wisdoms.

The arc of time measured by this collection begins far before Edoardo Ponti and his wife know of the child who will be coming to them. The poems of *Letters from a Young Father* necessarily become poems of memoir as well, a casting back to the poet's own childhood and early adulthood, enfolding stories and details of his personal history—not only his family history but also the profound and deeply compelling love story of Edoardo Ponti and his wife, the mother of the child he addresses.

Letters from a Young Father is a book of treasured reckonings, recollections and reflections not only about the family the poet has grown up within but also—perhaps most importantly—about the family he is making.

Edoardo Ponti asks: What makes a family? What are or will be the most sustaining elements that he, the poet-as-the-son, might carry with him as he moves toward this unknown role of being a new father, of being the son-as-a-father? Necessarily, he reflects passionately upon the presences of his own father and his own mother, recalling powerfully what they have given to him in the life leading to this moment.

Just as crucially, the poems of *Letters from a Young Father* emerge as spare epistles in which Edoardo Ponti searches for any lasting understanding that he might pass along to his child as he considers the dimensions and dilemmas of our existence in a complex world. He offers his own experience interwoven with loving and modest notes of instruction about those ways one might choose to live ethically and faithfully in this world.

Letters from a Young Father is one of the most heartbreakingly beautiful books of recent years. If I were to choose just one book to give to a new father or to a new mother at the beginning of his or her journey to becoming a parent, it would be, without question, Edoardo Ponti's *Letters from a Young Father.*

—David St. John

BEFORE THE BEGINNING

I.

You are not the first
The sun has kissed nor the last

But we will hold you and kiss you
Like the very first and the very last

No wind has blown through your hair
No ground has touched your feet

But you are in our every step
& all the air

You are still beyond time
But in our eyes you *are* already forever

Neither boy nor girl
We raise your tiny heart to the sun

& offer the promise of you to the sky
To the earth & to the wind

Let them bless those fresh first heartbeats
Those tiny knocks on our door

Born from courage
And the faith

Of this new soul called
You

II.

Before the beginning there was
A morning overlooking the Pacific
A small room with open windows
Sunlight softened by a veil of clouds

Before the beginning there was
A ring of coffee mugs on the bedside table
Silence of skin spreading through sheets
Eyes reading the movements of shadows

Before the beginning there was
A man and a woman with no map to connect
A chance meeting—A number
On a napkin and the first phone call

Before the beginning there was
Paris and pain—There was the courage to love
The blind leap of faith not so blind after all
Before the beginning

There was your mother—There was me
And all the false starts
That paved our separate ways
So we could find each other

Before the beginning
There was another world—A whole other me
Before the beginning
There was already you

WEEK 3 *(At home, watching the leaves)*

Was waiting in the waiting room but I already knew
Your mother walked out of the office
We embraced
That's what you do
At home we lay naked
I rested my hand on her belly
I spoke to her navel—That's what you do
She laughed
That's what you do

Got up to the bathroom—closed the door
Ran water in the sink so she couldn't hear my hands shake
No strength to take a deep breath
No desire to exhale
Just enough self-esteem to
Wash my face
That's what you do

Stood by the bathroom door
Watched your mother on her side
The rim of her ribs rising against the sunlight
The curve of her spine like a sine wave
Held her from behind
That's what you do

She took my hand—pressed it against her chest
She was crying but I kept quiet
Slid my foot between hers
My knee cupped her bent leg
The sun set—the room slipped into near dark

The lights of the city against our skin
My lips on her shoulder I whispered
I'm scared
She nodded—That was enough
That's what you do

WEEK 4 (*Holding a jasmine blossom*)

For you to dawn
Why does she need to dusk
For you to blossom
Why does she need to wither
Your mother has left her self
As abruptly as a sharp right
Silence is her new language
Sleep her new dance
She tries to hide her tears but I
Feel them in the absence of her touch
The only certainty is the fullness of her doubts
The only truth
That she knows nothing anymore
She tries to find a way back
But only sinks deeper
How much of her has to die to pay
For the beginnings of you
How much of our love do we have to give up
To feed your heart

Week 5 *(After rain)*

She took out the flowers but
Left water in the vase
Now it has stolen the colour of the petals
& not even candles can burn the smell
Of wet earth

I open the windows but there is so much
Unsaid the air has a hard time
Seeping into the house—So I walk out
Practice speaking to the sky
The wind answers—So does the rain
But not her

I wish I could peel away
My own darkness
But there is no space for my questions
Or fears—Only hers
Why can't we find answers together

The only bridge we have left
Is the memory of our eyes after love after you
She didn't say it that morning but
Her eyes knew what we had made
Those are the eyes I hang on to

Now that I'm leaving
She will kiss me good bye
Whisper I love you—But
Only the morning after love after you
Will carry me through work

That morning & you
Are the only flowers I have left

WEEK 6 (*Up 'til 5*)

My plane landed after the sun
Traffic tangled like cotton wool
Three messages—not one from her
At home the trees are empty
So is the house
The lights all off &
On the table a beet salad with a bowl of sliced fruit

I am alone in the dark
Coat on
Luggage at my feet like a pair of dogs
I eat then dial
I leave no message
  Where are we going
  What are we going to do
No answers but a tiny voice from across the room

I turn & see
Your mother in nightgown in shadow
The light of the streetlamp echoed in the tear balancing
On the lip of her eye like an acrobat on a tightrope
She whispers my name
Again
Without moving
The tear falls when she whispers
  I want to make love

Without moving I stand
Without moving we meet halfway
Without moving I take her face in my hands

The eyes are hers—The skin is hers
The way she takes me
In her arms without moving
The smell is hers

We kiss like the first time
No words no silence just the relief of pain gone
My skin praying the same appeal over and over again
As we make love
     Marry me
She smiles without moving
I see the night ripple
She answers without moving

WEEK 7 *(Second office to the left)*

We will never forget
The first time we saw you

Nothing but grains of grey
On the ultrasound monitor

Shifting shapes like canyons of shadows
Or liquid landscapes until

The doctor points
To a tiny mass in the screen corner

A swirling cloud of cells over all the noise
And in the middle a blinking light

Like a distant lighthouse throwing
Her line into a snowstorm

That pulsating glow
That is the beginning of your heart

So before skin
And bone

Before there is a beat to hear
Or an organ to monitor

Before there is life
There is this lighthouse burning through a snowstorm

Your own light will be born from it
As will the expression in your eyes

It was you before there was you
Who we made and who we first saw

WEEK 8 (*In medias res*)

At night
The rain hit the roof
Like a school of pointed fingers
The morning after
I walked out on the balcony
The sun was near complete
& every roof top
Was unfurling sheets of white smoke
I ran to my mother
She didn't understand my cry
      Was she blind
        Every house was on fire
        & the sky stealing their colour
She didn't laugh but I could hear
The tickle in her voice
It wasn't fire she explained
But sun melting dew into steam
& that arch in the sky
Was called a *rainbow*
        How can a bow shoot colour
I hid in my mother's arms all morning
Couldn't have been older than seven

This afternoon your mother sent me out for pickles & cream
No strange request for a woman expecting
Coming back home
The light hitting an exhaust fume
Reminded me of my mother's voice
With those eyes and that smile

The smell of her love made me cry
And so grateful to be alive

Week 9 (*Minutes before Monday*)

A blank body of water
Is how we all begin
Clear—Untouched
Then one dye after the next
One day after the next
One shade for every moment
Seeps into our fabric
As many pigments as there are memories
Dreams & regrets
Gradually your history paints the water
Shades will shift
But what matters
At the finish line
Is the final hue
That's the colour your children will wear
When you think your life has turned grey
Reminding you how empty
The water was in the beginning
& how far you've come
Without realizing it

WEEK 10 (*Stuck in traffic*)

Never give to receive
Or kiss to be kissed

Never hold to be held
Or love to be loved

Your light does not live
In the eyes of others

But in the peace of your palm
When you give just to give

It lives on the lip of your lips
When you kiss just to kiss

On the tip of your touch
When you hold just to hold

In the abandon of your heart
When you love just to love

& if you follow this with the simplicity
Only wisdom may bring

Then all the light you spread
Will be returned

Week 11 (*In bed, hearing the shower in the bathroom*)

This is the name game we play
Your mother and me
When the walls are asleep
& the rug hasn't stretched out like the cat that it is

When we hear nothing but
The sugar in the coffee and the
Butter on the bread
We pretend you are late for school
& in the empty house
As casual as possible
We call out a name

From the exhumed archaics—The impossible exotics
To the invisible regulars & sunburnt contemporaries
Most fall by the wayside
But those that stick
Ring with a faint echo
In the quiet house
Like the walls bouncing back
The whisper of our future memories

This is the name we look for
A name you could butter bread with
And sugar coffee
A name already so deeply baked into
The bones of our home
All we need
Is to listen for it

WEEK 12 (*In the elevator before my 11 o'clock*)

There is so much I want
For your life

The peace to sleep with both eyes
& wake with the wealth to realize

You don't need much
Just the wisdom to stay around long enough

To understand
& accept the unexpected

Ask me any question
Like why I failed when there was no reason

Or why I fell when I had the blueprint to all the traps
I promise I will answer

Even if it means you will respect me less
& if one day you are old enough to understand

All my failures and disappointments
Will have been worth something

WEEK 13 (*In the front seat, waiting for your mother*)

Funny—not sure why I remembered
At the doctor's office
My father when I was three
Coming home from a business trip
Your uncle & I waiting for him in our
Slippers downstairs—The ringing of the key
& that funny squeak when the tall oak door opened
Like a bearded giant wearing a girl's voice
He threw his scarf onto the black hanger
Silk whistling against metal
& thumped the striped suitcase onto
The marble floor to receive us in his arms

I remember the leather luggage unlatched
Your uncle's smile holding his new toy
I remember waiting for mine & before
My father realized he'd forgotten
I pretended running to the bathroom for a pee
But really hiding behind my bedroom door
To spare him the embarrassment—That night
I laughed through dinner to hold back the tears
Kissed my father good night more than once
To make sure he knew I loved him anyway
I did such a good job
He never noticed his oversight & did it again
More than once

Funny—not sure why the memory struck when I saw you
Not sure what we were expecting on the monitor
A tiny tadpole or less but there you were

Only a few cells big but so realized already—Facing us
With limbs open to receive us & eyes so clear
Staring right into my own—I tried to laugh
But this time I could not hold back the tears
Of all the surprises I expected & never got
You were the first I got without expecting

WEEK 14 *(At a train stop)*

In life my love
Hang on to the sail of your passions

When the wind is a wall of no
Be the yes that shifts the currents

The breath that turns an ember
Back into a raging fire

The only hull that holds course
When the cynics divert the stream

The steam that slices up
& gives body to your battle cry

& should your waves tire or lose their way
Know that I will always be there

A still and quiet shore to crash on

WEEK 15 (*On the leaking porch*)

Some say babies are born blind
But the truth is
Right after birth
They lock eyes with the first person they see
This look of disarming surrender
Unconditional & selfless
Is what welds us
Is the reason our hearts manage to beat
Even when we are asleep or forget we have a heart

It is with these eyes we should try & welcome
All those nameless faces in the street
Every single one of them sons & daughters
So they may remember the first look they gave when
They became sons & daughters & those eyes
That answered back

My love
The time approaches when our gazes will meet
& though you too will forget
Remember my words
So one day
You can dust off those eyes & offer them
To your worst enemy
We all deserve the chance to return the gift
With the same courage and simplicity
No matter whether the promise
Will last one blink
Or a lifetime

WEEK 16 (*Beside your mother asleep on the sofa*)

To amnio or not to amnio
To sink a needle into your mother's belly
To suck fluid from the only world you know
(Already we take)
& to crystal ball it for future defects
That's the question
The risk is a miscarriage—The reward
The assurance you are not broken
Because there is a zero point six per cent chance you might be
Odds even the meekest of gamblers would grab
Odds we can't afford because we are afraid
That's all
We are ready to risk a miscarriage because
We are afraid you'll fall in that zero point six per cent
Fear blinding us from the fact that
There is a ninety-nine point four per cent chance
You are perfectly unbroken
(Already we gamble)

WEEK 17 (*After a phone call with mammina*)

Falling in love
As a kid I didn't know
What it meant

But the image haunted me—of
two people meeting
& tumbling heart first

In a hole of
their own feeling
Never to be found

(I'm sure Phil Collins
Was partly to blame)
But for the longest time

I avoided all eye contact
So I wouldn't disappear
In a hole burrowed by love

It lasted 'til I was eight
God knows how many opportunities
Slipped by

    But today I wish you lift
    Your gaze and meet
    As many eyes as you can

As often as you can
So you can fall hard
As hard as you can

Love may hurt like death
But it's the only pain
That will truly make you feel alive

That and slow dancing to Phil Collins

Week 18 *(A thought watching TV)*

Regret

Tears at your toes
Gnaws at your elbows
Wraps an armpit 'round your nose
Try to breathe

Regret

Is seasickness on land
Hope played backwards
A pocketful of future
With a hole in it

Regret

Is a star
Having given up searching
For a night sky to wear

Regret

Is the only echo you have left
When you've been hollowed out

Regret

Will run you dry & leave you bankrupt
Unless you belt up
& pay your dues to your dreams

Owe nothing to regret
Don't be late
Don't be greedy
Live

That's all you owe your mother & me

WEEK 19 (*Can't sleep*)

We did the amnio
But no matter its good sense
We failed you
We believed in the odds and not in you
Listened to science—Not ourselves

A needle in your mother to determine
How disposable you are
A needle that came so close to your thigh
You moved away
I saw it—I saw the needle and did nothing to stop it
I felt your mother's hand tighten
I did nothing to stop it
Because in this world my Sun
Numbers have displaced Destiny
Science is stronger than soul
& we let ourselves be led
By the drumbeat of *just in case*

& just like that
The liquid was stolen—tested
& all was fine
The numbers were wrong—You
All right
But that night I couldn't sleep
Kept up by the one question
I didn't want to answer
What if the numbers had been right

WEEK 20 (*After blowing out my birthday candles*)

We rise—We fall
Questions precede every step
Seduced by the carrot stick of answers
My father used to say
Answers are not the answer
It's the question that counts
Instead of wasting away
Searching for answers
Have the courage
To find meaning without them
True meaning
Is understanding rather than knowing
Understanding that
Although you will never hold all the whys or the wherefores
You can live deeply and faithfully nonetheless

So when someone asks you a question
I don't know
Is often the best reply

　　When you let go
　　You begin

WEEK 21 (*While swimming, this memory*)

As you grow older
Life narrows like an iris shot with light
My father's whole existence became the carousel
Of three memories—This is my favourite
> When I was a boy after the war
> I would walk through the skeletons of old villages
> Bathing in the pink and clay bones of
> Tiny towns teetering
> On cliff tops like trapeze artists
> One late afternoon I met an old man
> In an old orchard
> Bent over those peaches that had
> Decided to meet the earth
> He turned them over
> Delicately one by one
> Like jewels with a heartbeat
> So the skin of each
> Would receive its ration of sun
> I watched 'til something in me
> Could not resist the question
>> Does God exist
> The old man turned
> Like he had been born and had lived
> One thousand lives just for this moment
> He took one breath full of peach
> And replied
>> Listen
>> To say that God exists might be a lie
>> But to say He doesn't is an even bigger one
> & just like that

He returned to his earth
Like he had been born and lived
One thousand lives for this orchard
For his peaches
For this question

WEEK 22 (*On a napkin with a broken pencil*)

Tonight I fell asleep
Listening to the wind lend
Voice to the leaves
Watching the snow dress
The trees & strip earth of all sound
For the first time I felt what it meant
To belong
Holding you & your mother from behind
Like another backbone just in case
While we were resting
The world continued
Snow swelled the garden
& you grew that one extra cell
Just enough of a tickle
To wake your mother—She gasped
I smiled but kept my eyes closed
So forever I could remember this moment
A dream dressed in snow

WEEK 23 (*A hard day & now this*)

When you think all is lost
Just remember this

    Your hands touch by mistake
        The world is saved

    You take a quiet walk down a crowded street
        The world is saved

    You connect with a stranger
        The world is saved

    You let it rain
        The world is saved

    You close your eyes to see more clearly
        The world is saved

    You give when you got nothing left
        The world is saved

    You let your silence speak
        The world is saved

    You knock even though the door won't open
        The world is saved

    You tell the truth when the lie is less painful
        The world is saved

You fall
    The world is saved

You get back up
    The world is saved

You say yes
    The world is saved

You are born
    The world is saved

WEEK 24 (*In the rearview mirror*)

What will I do with this world
With the raw and the right
The ugly and the good
What will your eyes touch first
How will I guide you through the unguidable
Today
Driving your mother
I took the roses way back home
Because you were in the car
I don't know why
It just felt right driving down
The perfumed side of the street with my family
     (Sometimes I shave before I speak to the belly of you
     Or wear a special sweater to the ultrasound
     I know it's silly but the thought of you
     Beckons me to seek what's light in the world
     & since it's so often hard to find
     My Sunday sweater will have to do)

WEEK 25 (*Light while I write*)

Papa
Why don't you have hair
On your head

Dinner froze
Silverware suspended
Chewing on mute
Mom's eyes lowered so she
Could sink her laugh
My brother bit his lip
But Dad didn't skip a beat
> *Would you rather have a full head of hair*
> *Or a full head of dreams*

One day you will ask me the same question
And I will answer you word for word
So my love
If you're a boy
No hair plugs
Use your grandfather's line instead
It'll save you money on surgery & painkillers
& if you're a girl
Don't discount a bald man for his follicular deficiencies
I promise what he lacks in hair
He'll make up for in dreams

Week 26 (*That song made me do it*)

Listen when I tell you
The moment you fall in love
Close your eyes & let go
If you pretend to be
The master of your heart
Then no matter how high the castle
You will only feel the depth of its moat
So get out of the way
Let life guide you
Whoever it is
Wherever
Whatever the price
Reach out to them with abandon
Love truthfully
And faithfully
Because if you don't
You'll end up
Sharing your days with someone
Who reminds you of the one
You were born to die for
& that's not living

WEEK 27 (*And this other song made me do this*)

We wait for the moment
We'll care about how you turn out

But until now
No desire to decipher

The height of your cheekbones
Or the colour of your eyes

Stunned by this indifference
And cautiously pleased

We reserve the right
To wake up one morning

Perfectly obsessed
With your looks

Meanwhile we hope to stay
Just the way we are

Peacefully detached
And already in love with

Just the way you are
But you already know our song

Week 28 (*In Zürich in transfer*)

If only there was armour
For all the advice arrowed our way
A secret shield against
All the catapulted tips
From all those who say they love us
But only really love the idea of telling us what to do
Like a dog likes bone
Only for him only for now
No we haven't read all the books
No we haven't baby-proofed every corner
No we haven't enrolled you in preschool
Your mother and I are just
Wasting valuable weeks
Eating and sleeping
Being and dreaming
& if one day you find
Your life was ruined for attending the wrong preschool
Or your self-esteem shot because the other parents
Knew more about the Brazelton technique
Then it's on us
But if you end up happy and whole because
You were raised by a man and a woman who loved you the way
They love each other
Who listened to you as much as they hear one another
Then please write to
All those who reveled in our incompetence
Tell them you forgive them
Because love has taught you that too

WEEK 29 (*With the ultrasound in my wallet*)

Not sure if it was a dream
Or a loud thought
Last night I saw you in my arms
No matter my funny faces
Wide smiles or silly songs
You looked away
More drawn to a crack in the ceiling
Than your father

It was only when I gave up my antics
That you landed your toothless grin on me
With your perfect cheeks & long eyelashes
I just needed to be myself for you to
Pay attention

So I promise
I will learn from the squeaky door
The wobbly table and the cracked ceiling
They are what they are
And I too will be what I am
Without the artifice the show or the sheen
I admit the mask was safer but
So be it
You'll get me how you want
Squeaks cracks wobbles and all

WEEK 30 (*Hearing laughter across the street*)

It was the tail of summer
The sun tasted like jasmine
The air ablush with the smell of
Long afternoons spent by the pool
Your uncle was nine
& asked your grandmother with
The index finger pointed to the sky
Like this one finger could pause
The Earth and switch off the sun
He asked her
Why do people have to die

My mother looked at him
With eyes like open arms
She took his finger with both hands
So the world could resume spinning & whispered
There are questions that only exist
To be asked
Never answered

Your uncle looked at the answer shining
Through this powerful delicate woman
He raised his finger at *her* this time
Then at himself
& leapt back in the pool

My mother returned to her magazine
Me to my inflatable fish
& one of the great lessons
Came and went in the jasmine sun
Of a summer long long ago

Week 31 *(Two days after April Fools')*

I wonder what you'll think of me
In my moments of weakness
With what eyes you will look at me
If I fail
With what voice you'll call me out
If I lie
Will you love me no matter what
Or will your heart have a floor

You don't have to like me
Because I know you love me
Is what I heard a mother yell
At her screaming son

I don't want to hide behind entitlements
Love is not inevitable
I want to earn my corner in your heart
Fight for my seat at your table
And the privilege to show up
Without reservation
Whenever I feel
Because that's also how you feel

A child is not given to a parent
Only lent
Is what I heard another mother say

I like the idea of treating you
Like a precious rental
One which eventually reverts back

To its rightful owner
Hopefully intact
Possibly enhanced

WEEK 32 (*In Geneva, in a cab*)

Last night
I held my father's hand
I held it so long so deep
His lines grew into my lines
& his sweat became mine

Last night
I held my father's breath
I held it so long so deep
His chest grew into my chest
& his heart became mine

Last night
I held my father's gaze
I held it so long so deep
His eyes grew into my eyes
& his life became mine

Last night my love
My father became mine
Outside it stopped raining
The moonlight melted the last of the sky
Last night

No fanfare or cry
Ninety-three years gone by
With one last heartbeat so faint
Even the moonlight was louder
& that was all

As humble as a secret
As quiet as the mystery of you
There is no difference
Between the beginning
Of life & the beginning of death

The first heartbeat
As indistinct as the last
So promise me my Sun that in the middle
You'll make as much noise as you can
For as long as you can

WEEK 33 (*Day for night with a moon so full*)

Wait 'til you meet your mother's eyes
She laid them on me over lunch today
And there was nothing left
But to rest my fork

In the quiet courage of her lines and this love
Like a spring leaf so fragile so translucent
No storm would ever be thick or passionate
Enough to tear or burn a hole through

Then this dimple of hers so precious
It could only be issued on one cheek
Embossed by freckles (I pray you have that too)
When she smiles her cheek turns to pastry
No other word for it

Her hands are tiny but always there
Her legs chiseled by the memory
Of skating—That balance
Which taught her how to fall

Then you'll meet her mouth
The kisses of which
Ground and levitate you
Like she invented the act

But enough said and maybe it's already too much
I can't wait to discover her through your eyes
Can't wait to meet the woman through your love
And the man I'll be with you both

WEEK 34 (*Back on the TGV*)

Now that I watch your mother dreaming in sleep
Rocked by the rhythm of the train
Head against the window
Wide fields pouring past us
It all looks so inevitable
But in case you don't remember
You came to us once before
In Paris one afternoon
Your mother felt funny
She went to the pharmacy &
Came out positive
All of a sudden nothing was the same
Not the sky spreading Spring
Not the Seine caught with light
Not even us

We took a walk instead
No hand holding so no thoughts
Only one look when we found
Ourselves in a store I don't remember
& together we inquired separately if
That hat in blue satin came in brown
We left without an answer & sat
On a bench facing traffic
To blur the hollowness but the hollowness never left

Until you did
The morning of a week later when
Blood woke your mother &
The hollowness turned to pain

The pain to realize that you left because
We were not ready
But that was enough to tear the mask off all
The fear hiding behind
Those meticulous manicured voices
Wagging their reasons *why not* instead of
What if
& once we understood this
You came back & we

> Are once again in Paris
> On the same train
> In the same room
> With the same footsteps
> On the same bench
> Sharing the same silence
> Not of hollowness this time
> But wholeness

The wholeness that comes with peace
The peace behind the leap of faith
The faith we touched when we rested our
Hands over your mother's belly
& on that park bench in Paris
Blessed you as best we could &
Thanked you for having granted us
This second chance

Week 35 (*Written in one breath*)

When nighttime sinks our eyes
& the city lights hum through the window
I quietly inch myself towards your mother
I wrap my arms 'round her belly
& you become the world

All day she carries you
But it is at night that we connect
It is at night that I receive a taste of your story
I lay my head against your mother's back
So I can hear your heartbeats through her bones
In Morse code you send me your secrets
One hundred and thirty-two a minute

Then like a blind man I read the Braille
Of your movements underneath the belly
& they become my only landscape
The short kick—The long shift   The quick poke
Is this your head
Was that a thigh or maybe an arm
Shapes & turns—Angles & waves
You have every body—you are every position
And with my eyes closed
The rhythm of my
Fingers read the person you will be
& nothing else matters

WEEK 36 (*Right before walking in*)

You will fall
    Life will go on

Your heart will break
    Life will go on

You will lose
    Life will go on

All I can tell you is this
Wear these moments with dignity
The way one wears an impossible medal
Because the taller the hurdle
The deeper Life's belief
You can clear it

So when Pain overwhelms you
Be flattered
When Injustice befalls you
Be flattered
When Life seems to turn against you
Be flattered
It's Her way of showing
How much faith She has

Week 37 (*Watching your mother apply lipstick*)

Three weeks to go
Can't wait to feel the weight of you in my arms
To walk you to burp you
I can't wait to speak to you
And know you feel me though
You don't understand one word
I can't wait for that mouth
To learn to smile
& that dimple peeking through the trials
I can't wait to dive into the smell of your breath
When you yawn after milk
Because in the beginning it will be the smell of you
That will speak to us
That will tell us you are ours
Before the words and the sounds
The scent of new skin
And a heart finding its place
I can't wait to hear you breathe
Against my chest and those tiny lungs
Deepening with sleep after sunset
I can't wait to call your name
Without noticing anymore
I can't wait to push my thumb in the palm of your hand
So you may grab it
At first only a reflex but then knowing
Whose thumb you are holding
Three weeks to go twenty-one days 1440 hours
Don't rush but hurry
So I can share my life with you

And call every day after the first
Yours

WEEK 38 (*Watching a gardener blow leaves off my deck*)

Remember
There is nothing romantic
In declaring eternal love—First
It's a lie because death
Gets in the way
But most of all
Love isn't length
It's risk—The risk of
Packing all that is dearest
And handing it over to
The chosen one
Without deposit
Without warranty
Without receipt
Only the trust your faith
Has put in them
That leap is love
The stakes you need
To keep a marriage from shrinking
Because if the wholeness of your heart
Depends on the wholeness of the one
Entrusted with it
You will do everything you can
To make sure they don't lose interest
Is it scary
Yes
Worth it
Of course and
Far more exciting

Besides
Life's too short
Love shouldn't feel like
Forever

Week 39 (*Watching her smile*)

When I was four
I took my first flight
& when we pierced through the clouds
There was the blue & *there* was the sun

As soon as we landed
I wanted to reveal the secret
To all those who were blue
No need to let bad weather reports
Mar our mood
When above rain
The sun was shining without a blink

When I shared my discovery
Nobody cared
For all they knew
Was the grey they could see

I long for the moment
You will run to me
With the same light
In your eyes

I will listen so you can have
The pleasure to teach me and I
The pleasure to show you
How much I believe

Week 40 (*In the waiting room with both grandmothers*)

You want to know how it feels

You want to know how it feels
To hold in your arms a body full of
Your blood—A face full of your eyes
A smile full of your smile
And two tiny feet walking
On the palm of your hand

It is the quiet hum of a new star
The secret whisper of first snowfall
Warm water on morning skin
No symphonic explosion
Or shattering epiphany
It is a corner of light that grows
Silently imperceptibly
Illuminating at last everything
You already knew
Without ever having proof
Until now

Outside the wind has picked up
It's snowing bougainvillea petals
Welcome my child
Welcome my world
I looked into your eyes
& found my life
Now it is my turn to listen

After All

I.

Hold him
Hold him

My dear and only father
I promise I will try and forgive

All the love you buried in secret corners of you
Without ever finding the blueprint to our arms

Hold her
Hold her

My dear and only mother
You loved us with the might and sacrifice of a general

You won all the wars with little peace left in your heart
But always so much faith

II.

After all
This is through you

After all
This is from you

After all
This is in you

Sasha
You gave me your life

With the purity of a glass of water
I will spend the rest of mine

Making sure I won't spill a drop

BIOGRAPHICAL NOTE

Edoardo Ponti is a film director who divides his time between California and Italy. The son of Sophia Loren and producer Carlo Ponti, Edoardo has written and directed numerous award-winning feature films and shorts, as well as plays and an opera. Edoardo Ponti graduated magna cum laude from the University of Southern California in 1994 with a BA in creative writing. He went on to earn an MFA in film directing and production from USC's prestigious School of Cinematic Arts in 1997. Edoardo is married to the actress Sasha Alexander, with whom he has two wonderful children. This is his first book of poetry.

Printed in the USA
CPSIA information can be obtained
at www.ICGtesting.com
JSHW080007150824
68134JS00021B/2326